9/1

To all

thank you

being there alright

May you always

be gracious and

caring!

love
Beverly

Diane

T0649014

allison Applehans

Creating Caring Children

Copyright © 2002 by the Grace Contrino
Abrams Peace Education Foundation

All rights reserved. No part of this publication
may be reproduced or transmitted in any form
or by any means, electronic or mechanical,
including photocopy, recording, or any
information storage and retrieval system,
without permission in writing from
the publisher.

Requests for permission to make copies of
any part of this work should be mailed to the
following address: Permissions Department,
Peace Education Foundation, 1900 Biscayne
Boulevard, Miami, Florida 33132-1025
(305) 576-5075 or (800) 749-8838

www.PeaceEducation.com

Library of Congress Number: 2002107463

Creating Caring Children; The First Three
Years/Diane Carlebach and Beverly Tate,
with Illustrations by Miguel Luciano—1st ed.

ISBN 1-878227-86-6

Edited by James Burke II
Book and cover design by Ron Dilley
Illustrations by Miguel Luciano
Proof reader Sister Lucy Coressel, O.P.

Creating Caring Children

The First Three Years

by
Diane Carlebach
and
Beverly Tate

Illustrations by
Miguel Luciano

With a foreword by David Lawrence, Jr.

PeaceWorks
Peace Education ™
F O U N D A T I O N

Acknowledgements

To my dear friend and colleague, Beverly, for her caring, compassion and knowledge. This project was a work from our hearts and a commitment to improving the lives of very young children. To my two babies, Adam and Joshua, now grown men. Thank you for showing me how exciting and beautiful "becoming" can be. To Dan for his consistent support, encouragement and love. — *Diane*

To Diane, my dear friend and colleague, who has the ability to transform everyday words and actions into beautiful expressions of care and love. You are the one who truly led us to this project and continually provided inspiration and clarity.

To my caring children Brantley, Justin and Whitney, and to my grandchildren, Braden, Kent and Mackenzie, the magical infants and toddlers who provide the inspiration and hope for a caring world. — *Beverly*

Thank you to all our supporters, editors and collaborators, without whose help this book would not be here: John Mazzarella, Lloyd Van Bylevelt, James Burke, Ron Dilley, Chuck Bryant, Marta Moreno, Frank Vega, Sister Marie Carol Hurley, O.P., Gail Neumann and Susan Gold. To Barbara Edwards, whom we love and who supports what we do with sincere enthusiasm. And to those who inspired us: David Lawrence, Magda Gerber, Dr. Becky Bailey and Janet Gonzalez-Mena.

The Peace Education Foundation would like to thank the Allegany Franciscan Foundation, Dade County, Inc., for its generosity and support. We would also like to thank the Kiwanis Club of Miami for its generous donation.

Table of Contents

Table of Contents

Foreword

For years I've known how important it is to build great elementary and secondary schools, how important it is to build a world-class higher education system. But not until a few years ago did I come to realize that greatness can never fully emerge from students who didn't get a good start. I have come to believe that one of the wisest possible uses of our resources is time and money spent on children from birth to age five. I have come to believe that the future of our community and our country depends on children getting off to a strong start in life.

Only a few years ago, I was among the many who had no idea how important readiness is; the matter of brain research had never crossed my mind. But I am now aware of the "explosion of learning" that occurs right after birth. My reading has led to such books as Alison Gopnik, Andrew N. Meltzoff and Patricia K. Kuhl's *The Scientist in the Crib: Mind, Brains and How Children Learn* and this excerpt: "What we see in the crib is the greatest mind that has ever existed, the most powerful learning machine in the universe. The tiny fingers and mouth are exploration devices that probe the alien world around them with more precision than any Mars Rover. The crumpled ears take a buzz of incomprehensible noise and flawlessly turn it into meaningful language. The wide eyes that sometimes seem to peer into your very soul actually do just that, deciphering your deepest feelings. The downy head surrounds a brain that is forming millions of new connections every day."

Predicated on that image and that science, I came to realize that it is simply tragic that so many children start formal school so significantly behind where they ought to be.

This is neither a matter of politics nor party—and should not be. It is everyone's "business." Recall the Congressional testimony not long ago of First Lady Laura Bush: "There simply is no excuse for any of our youngest and most vulnerable children to be forced to climb uphill just as they enter school," she said.

"School readiness" is *not*, of course, about children learning to read by age three. The fact that your child or grandchild can read at age five, four or even three does not make him or her per se smarter than other people's children. Rather, school "readiness" is about children growing—socially, emotionally, physically, intellectually and, yes, spiritually—so that they are ready and eager to learn by the time they reach first grade. It *is* about the blending of education and health and nurturing in the earliest years.

Erase those images of tiny children—three-year-olds—in tiny desks with a teacher at the blackboard. Rather, imagine our youngest children learning in a fuller, different context. See the crucial nature of "teachable moments" in a child's earliest years.

Our mission must embrace what Dr. Martin Luther King, Jr. spoke of: "*all* of God's children." All children need all the quality early care and education that your children and my own need: Love and nurturing. All their shots. Excellent nutrition. The fullest opportunity to be safe. Stimulating Pre-K. Childcare that engages the mind, not the "warehousing" that most children receive. "What the wisest and best parents want for (their) own children, (so) must the community want for all its children," said educator John Dewey. And author James Baldwin wrote: "For these are all our children.... We will all profit by, or pay for, whatever they become."

How much more research do we need to tell us what we already know? On the power of "language development" in the first two years, for instance, I note the important new book called *Meaningful Differences,* by Drs. Betty Hart and Todd Risley. "We saw," they wrote, "that what parents said and did with their children in the first three years of language learning had an enormous impact on how many languages their children learned and used... We were awestruck at how well our measures of accomplishments at age three predicted measures of language skill at ages nine and ten... We learned from the longitudinal data that the problem of skill differences among children at the time of school entry is bigger, more intractable and more important than we had thought."

That brings me to this book, whose title, *Creating Caring Children,* seems so vital to what everyone would want for a child's early years. By explaining to parents and caregivers how to provide young children with appropriate, nurturing responses during the day-to-day situations they encounter, this book helps foster children's brain development. This brain development will in turn greatly affect children's ability to learn and succeed in school and in life. Its authors, Diane Carlebach and Beverly Tate, are caring professionals and community leaders. Both are steeped in the experience of early childhood development, care, compassion and education.

The publisher, Miami's Peace Education Foundation, has a long and distinguished record of service in the cause of harmony and justice.

David Lawrence, Jr.
President
The Early Childhood Initiative Foundation
Miami

Introduction

W hen caring for young children, adults sometimes focus upon one of two extremes: they try to placate children by letting them do whatever they please or suppress them with strict discipline and physical punishment.

While these approaches may affect children's behavior in the short-run, neither helps children develop valuable life skills such as self-confidence, social competence, compassion, assertiveness and non-violent problem-solving skills — the skills they will need to become successful, healthy adults.

Creating Caring Children does. *Creating Caring Children* provides parents and childcare professionals with safe, appropriate responses to common-yet-difficult conflict situations. These responses model assertive, problem-solving language and behaviors, and will help the infants and toddlers in the adult's care grow to become caring children who can resolve conflicts successfully and non-violently.

Creating Caring Children is written for caregivers and parents who want to take their relationships with their infants and toddlers to a higher level, for those who want not only to care for children, but also to mentor them. Modeling non-violent problem solving through language and behavior must be a priority for high-quality parenting and childcare. Spending this time and effort during these formative years will infuse in children healthy habits and life skills. Childcare centers and homes that implement these principles will be places where children can grow and learn peacefully and successfully.

The intent of *Creating Caring Children* is to focus on general behaviors as a means for adults to identify and model the characteristics we want children to develop. The more knowledge we have about our children, the more appropriate our responses to their behavior will be. In the infant and toddler years, young children need adults in their lives to be flexible, understanding, calm, sensitive, observant, knowledgeable, empathetic, and willing to converse, read, sing and laugh at the wonders of the world. Adults must develop many languages—verbal and nonverbal—with young children to create a foundation for future healthy relationships and a strong self-concept. They include the languages of:

+ empathy
+ problem solving
+ encouragement
+ acknowledging and describing feelings—theirs and yours
+ describing their world and their interactions

Nothing can substitute for quality parenting. However, with the number of two-career and single parent families at an all-time high, the need for childcare in recent years has increased dramatically. Unfortunately, quality childcare is not always easy to find. A recent study by the University of Colorado states that 40 percent of infant and toddler environments placed children's health and welfare at substantial risk. Among the risk factors cited were lack of warm supportive relationships with caring adults, and few materials that encourage social, physical, emotional and intellectual growth.

Creating Caring Children gives you a framework with which to provide quality care for children, add value to your childcare facility and give parents an added peace of mind. These practices help form the basis for literacy and academic success. Most importantly, however, *Creating Caring Children* helps you do your part to ensure that today's infants and toddlers become tomorrow's healthy, happy adults.

We cannot address every possible challenge or problem. Nor can we consider every cultural influence that affects exactly what a caregiver may say or do. In this book we provide a representative set of situations, emphasizing best practices and key principles based on current research and understanding. Focusing on key statements and principles helps caregivers respond to children's needs not impulsively out of frustration or irritation, but consciously, deliberately, and rationally out of our knowledge, awareness, and understanding.

We may use many different ways and words to nurture children. Interpret and apply these as best you can.

Chapter One 1

Infants need relationships to meet their basic human needs of attachment and survival. Relationships that are positive and healthy give infants a sense of trust and security. Adults who do not respond appropriately to babies' cues or signals may create unhealthy and negative relationships. Adults strengthen positive relationships by immediately engaging infants in "conversations"—speaking to them in soft tones, talking with them about every little event and process, verbalizing the answers that the infant might say, always recognizing and consciously describing the infant's abundant communication through facial expression, movement, and vocalizations. Making these conversations a constant practice not only establishes the caring and security that infants need, but also lays a rich foundation for language, literacy, and later academic success.

Healthy infants:

+ Are born ready to communicate and form relationships
+ Cry to communicate physical or emotional discomfort and "coo" to communicate pleasure
+ Begin to consciously return smiles at about two-and-one-half months
+ Recognize and respond to familiar people
+ Progress from involuntary to voluntary movement
+ Are physically and emotionally dependent on others
+ Need to move to develop their brains and bodies
+ Form routines that become identifiable and predictable

What infants need from adults:

+ Physical closeness, holding and touching
+ Responsiveness to cues or signals for engagement or disengagement
+ Time and space for independent movement
+ To hear familiar voices talking to them, which creates a sense of comfort and an opportunity to learn language
+ To have their cries and vocalizations understood and differentiated

On Your Tummy Before You're Ready

Supporting Physical Development

SITUATION:

Ivy, two months old, has been playing contentedly on her back on a quilt on the floor. When she begins to get fussy, the adult comes over and says, "You have been lying on your back for quite a while. Let's turn you on your tummy." The adult turns her over and puts a toy in front of her so she can look at it. Ivy tries to lift her head and struggles to get comfortable. As her head bobs up and down her fussiness increases.

COMMON ADULT RESPONSE:

"Ivy, you have to learn to be on your tummy. It will make your arms strong."

CONSCIOUS ADULT RESPONSE:

Caring and Descriptive Language:

The adult should go through a mental checklist when the infant is fussy. The checklist includes asking: **"Are you wet or hungry?" "Do you need me to talk to you, rock you, walk with you?" "Do you need to go to sleep?"**

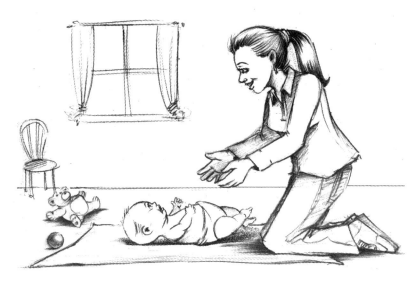

Sitting beside Ivy, start the conversation: **"Ivy, I hear you fussing, I am going to sit here with you."** Waiting for a response and quietly acknowledging her fussiness calms the interaction. If she calms down, you will know your closeness has met her need. If Ivy continues to fuss, say, **"Let's see if you want me to hold you."** If she continues to fuss, check her physical needs, diapering, room temperature, burp, etc.

Why Am I Doing This?

Young infants communicate their needs by fussing or crying. Adults need to respond and not ignore fussy babies. The work of the adult is to interpret the infant's need from a place of knowledge and caring.

Conceptual Framework:

Child's Point of View:

"I don't like being on my tummy yet!"

Why Does This Matter?

In order to appropriately meet the needs of young infants, adults must be responsive to the needs of young infants and knowledgeable about their physical development.

COMMON BEHAVIOR AND NORMAL DEVELOPMENT:

Putting Ivy in a position she cannot get into herself, *e.g.* rolling over onto her stomach, creates a sense of helplessness and discomfort. This deprives her of the opportunity to follow her natural physical development. Leaving Ivy on her back allows her to freely move her arms and legs strengthening her tummy muscles, which will drive her ability to turn herself over. When she can turn herself over by herself, her stomach muscles will be strong enough to support her in her position. She will be able to raise her body comfortably.

ATTITUDES THAT CREATE CARING COMMUNITIES:

✦ "I will trust and support your emerging physical development and not put you in positions for which you are not ready." (This refers to children without identified special needs.)

SKILLS FOR CONSCIOUS EVERYDAY RESPONSES:

✦ Respond to fussy infants with care and knowledge.

IF YOU NEED MORE:

Other conscious ways for the adult to stay objective and rational:

If you have gone through the mental checklist, given Ivy time to respond to each initiative, and given yourself time to read her responses, walking outside with the infant (weather permitting) often provides a calming effect.

Are You Going to Spoil Him?

Being Responsive to Create Relationships

SITUATION:

Anna has just finished feeding and burping Luqman, three months old, and is in the process of changing his diaper. After completing the diaper change, Anna places him on a quilt beside her while she sits and talks to her friend Joan. Luqman begins to get fussy. Anna gives Luqman her finger to hold, but he begins to cry. Anna says, "Oh, Luqman, you have been fussy for the last couple of days. What do you need?" Anna then moves to pick him up.

Common Adult Response:

"Let him be, Anna. If you pick him up every time he cries, you are going to spoil him."

Conscious Adult Response:

Caring and Descriptive Language:

For Anna and Luqman: Anna may be feeling frustrated because Luqman is fussy. If so, it is helpful to stop, take a deep breath and reflect on what worked in the past to comfort him, *e.g.,* rocking him. Rock him and say to him, **"Luqman, the last time you were fussy, I rocked you and you liked it. Let's try that again."** If the rocking does not work this time, choose another strategy, such as singing to him, talking to him in a soft, soothing voice, gently rubbing his arm or back, holding him close or walking him. The caregiver might say to Luqman, **"Rocking isn't comforting you this time. Let's try walking."**

Finally, don't give up. Identifying and internalizing a calming habit takes time and practice.

For Joan: Joan can offer support for Anna and Luqman, **"Let me know if you need my help with Luqman. My kids used to love it when I sang to them."**

WHY AM I DOING THIS?

It is essential for Luqman to feel connected to someone he trusts to help him find comfort. Time with a trusted adult and a consistent calming method will help Luqman create an avenue of comfort for himself. The earlier a child and his/her family or caregivers discover or develop the child's primary calming method, the earlier they are setting the foundation for self-calming behavior.

Describing what we are doing and why with young infants, *e.g.* "The last time you were fussy, I rocked you and you liked it," provides the infant with a verbal and physical connection to his or her caregiver. By talking to him, the caregiver is acknowledging the infant as a fellow human being with needs and feelings. This models self-talk, a processing method that helps people sort out and solve problems.

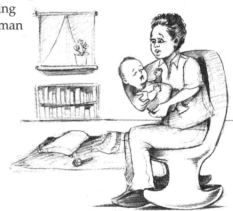

CONCEPTUAL FRAMEWORK:
Child's Point of View:

"I feel uncomfortable and I don't know what to do about it."

Why Does This Matter?

The caring conscious response develops Luqman's emotional security because the adult responds to his emotional needs. He learns to trust the adults in his world. He begins to experience how comfort feels. This is the first step in developing healthy methods of self-comfort as he grows.

COMMON BEHAVIOR AND NORMAL DEVELOPMENT:

Some infants have temperaments or physical conditions that require more opportunity to create trust or habits of comfort. The primary adults in an infant's life offer ways of finding comfort from which a child adopts his or her own method of feeling comforted. If the child is consistently comforted

by being rocked, walked, patted, or sung to, one or more of these caring actions will probably become the primary method that comforts him or her.

Children who are held often and comforted during the first year of life actually demand less attention later on because they have learned to trust the adults in their environment to meet their needs and give them comfort when necessary. Helping children learn to meet their own needs provides the foundation for emotional security. Therefore, holding a child who is in discomfort will not spoil him or her, but will in fact help the child become emotionally secure. Emotional security is the basis for a strong, socially competent child.

ATTITUDES THAT CREATE
CARING COMMUNITIES:

✦ "When you cry, I will know it is a signal that you need comfort."

SKILLS FOR CONSCIOUS
EVERYDAY RESPONSES:

✦ Rocking, walking, talking, gently rubbing and singing help infants find comfort.

IF YOU NEED MORE:

Other conscious ways for the adult to stay objective and rational:

You may grow physically or emotionally exhausted from dealing with a child who does not respond to your caring and conscious comforting. A break may be necessary to refuel your energies. Have strategies in place to deal with the situation:

1. Ask someone to take over for you for a while.

2. If no one else is around, put the infant down in a safe familiar place, speaking to the infant periodically so that he/she hears your voice. This keeps a connection between the two of you so that he/she does not feel abandoned. The caregiver might say, "Luqman, I am going to put you down now, but I will stay close by."

3. To get on with essential tasks of daily life, try using a "snuggly." This fabric sling allows you to strap the infant to your body, leaving your hands free.

4. Call a healthcare professional.

Diaper Changing

Routines as Interactions, Not Distractions

SITUATION:

The adult picks up four month old Lydia, says "Let's go, Lydia," and carries her to the diaper-changing table. As she lays Lydia down, she turns on the musical mobile hanging over the changing table, gives Lydia a rattle, and starts to sing the tune the mobile is playing.

COMMON ADULT RESPONSE:

The adult says "Lydia, look! The mobile is going around and around. Isn't it pretty?" as she begins to change the diaper.

Conscious Adult Response:

Caring and Descriptive Language:

The caring adult walks over to Lydia, sits down beside her and waits for Lydia to look at her/him. When Lydia acknowledges her/his presence, the adult says, "**Lydia, it is time for us to change your diaper.**" The adult holds out her/his arms, and waits for Lydia to respond, *e.g.*, make eye contact, make body movements, etc. The adult then picks Lydia up.

Moving toward the diaper-changing table, the adult says, "**We are going to the diaper-changing table. We will get your diaper and lay you on the pad.**"

The adult lays Lydia down on the pad, he/she says, "**Lydia, I am going to take off your wet diaper.**" The caring adult continues to describe each step in the diaper-changing process to Lydia. She/he should use as much eye contact as possible and pause momentarily before beginning each new step.

WHY AM I DOING THIS?

The time and attention given to this interactive diaper-changing process creates a greater sense of intimacy with Lydia. The caring adult who uses this type of interaction deepens her/his consciousness and understanding that diaper changing and other daily rituals are in fact valuable learning experiences for infants.

CONCEPTUAL FRAMEWORK:

Child's Point of View:

"I like to know what is happening to me."

Why Does This Matter?

The description of what is happening to Lydia as it happens creates a greater sense of trust with the caring adult because she is not caught off guard or surprised by the diaper change. She needs to be informed about what is happening to her, and to be directly connected and involved throughout the process without being distracted. When her attention remains on the caring adult throughout the process, it is a chance for their relationship to grow and strengthen. The routine and predictability of the diaper-changing process helps Lydia understand how others take care of her needs. This lays the foundation for the child to learn about caring for herself.

COMMON BEHAVIOR AND NORMAL DEVELOPMENT:

Infants have a basic need and motivation to create relationships. Adults meet this need with caring verbal and nonverbal communication, *e.g.*, describing what is happening to the infants, describing who is around them, telling them how much they love them, smiling at them, picking them up with a loving expression, etc. If their needs are met, they willingly engage in and respond to these verbal and nonverbal communications. They are hearing the sounds of language and beginning to participate in the turn-taking of conversation. This stage of development is commonly called "the falling-in-love period" because they are so open to connecting to the caring adults in their lives.

ATTITUDES THAT CREATE CARING COMMUNITIES:

✦ "I will take time with diaper changing so we can connect and strengthen our relationship."

SKILLS FOR CONSCIOUS EVERYDAY RESPONSES:

✦ Involve the infant by describing what is happening.

✦ Respect the infant by doing things *with* him/her and not *to* him/her.

✦ Watch for the infant's responses.

IF YOU NEED MORE:

Other conscious ways for the adult to stay objective and rational:

Assess the situation. If Lydia becomes fussy or starts to wiggle, the caring adult should speed up or slow down the diaper-changing process.

Taking Turns with Language

Building Relationships

SITUATION:

Lashandra is sitting with her five-month-old daughter, Laticia. Laticia begins to "coo" and smile. Lashandra says, "Laticia, you are talking to me." Laticia laughs aloud. Lashandra says, "You are such a happy girl. I love it when you smile." Laticia coos back to her mom. Lashandra keeps talking to the baby. Laticia turns her head and breaks eye contact with her mother.

COMMON ADULT RESPONSE:

Lashandra leans over so that she continues to be face to face with Laticia and continues to talk to her. "Laticia, look at mommy. Where did that smile go?"

CONSCIOUS ADULT RESPONSE:

Caring and Descriptive Language:

When Laticia turns her head away, she is indicating that she is ready to disengage from the conversation. **"Laticia, I love it when you talk to me, but I can tell you are ready to stop now."** Lashandra reads Laticia's cue of turning away and stops talking to her. She stays close, watching for Laticia to initiate eye contact again.

WHY AM I DOING THIS?

The turn-taking of conversations with infants builds intimacy and relationships. Talking with a baby models caring and effective communication. Babies hear the sounds of the language they will be speaking and feel accepted as a partner in the conversation.

CONCEPTUAL FRAMEWORK:
Child's Point of View:

"I don't want to talk anymore."

Why Does This Matter?

Growing and developing infants need to be connected with the adults in their life, but they also need time to be disconnected, as do adults. Adults who effectively read an infant's cues and respond accordingly are respecting the infant's need to connect or disconnect. Infants are learning to make sounds (the foundations of speech) and they need time, support and opportunity to practice their vocalizations. The adult who encourages these vocalizations with enthusiastic turn-taking is enhancing this development.

COMMON BEHAVIOR AND NORMAL DEVELOPMENT:

The essence of conversation is turn-taking, *e.g.*, I speak, you listen, then you speak and I listen. Turn-taking is possible only when the adult waits silently for the infant to respond. Eye contact indicates that the infant is interested and wants to be engaged. The turning of the head to the side or breaking eye contact indicates that the infant is ending the conversation for now.

Effective conversation with infants is based on describing what they are doing ("You are looking at me"), what is happening around them ("Oh, I hear a car driving up, I wonder who it is?"), how you feel about them ("I love you so much!"), and repeating the sounds they make.

ATTITUDES THAT CREATE CARING COMMUNITIES:

+ I know turn-taking is the basis for all conversation and it is possible and essential to have conversations with infants.

SKILLS FOR CONSCIOUS EVERYDAY RESPONSES:

✦ Watch for cues and responses.

IF YOU NEED MORE:

Other conscious ways for the adult to stay objective and rational:

Conversations with infants need to be natural and comfortable. This may take practice for some adults. Talk to infants the way you would to a friend. Practice as often as possible.

Begin reading to infants and make conversations about the stories. Even in the first year of life, this stimulates the brain connections that promote spoken language and eventual literacy.

Separation Anxiety

Taking Time with Transitions

SITUATION:

Zhu, eight months old, and his parents arrive at the childcare center. The two caregivers, who are standing inside the doorway talking to each other, greet the parents and Zhu. They ask the parents to put Zhu on the floor. As the parents try to set him comfortably on the quilt, Zhu begins to cry and reach for them. One of the caregivers notices the parents' anxious looks.

COMMON ADULT RESPONSE:

"Oh, don't worry about Zhu. He will be fine. Just leave him there. He always stops crying after you leave."

CONSCIOUS ADULT RESPONSE:

Caring and Descriptive Language:

The primary caregiver welcomes Zhu with open arms and eye contact to connect with him and to gauge his readiness to leave his parents. The caregiver might say, **"Good morning, Zhu. I have been waiting for you. Would you like me to hold you while Mom and Dad put your things away?"**

If Zhu resists, the caregiver must acknowledge his resistance. The caregiver might say, **"Zhu, I can see you are not ready to say good-bye yet,"** and then walk with Zhu and the parents to the quilt. With parents, caregiver and Zhu on the quilt, they can take a moment to share important information, *e.g.,* when he ate last, how he slept.

When it is time for the parents to leave, say to Zhu, **"Mom and**

Dad have to go to work, so you are going to be with me now.
They will come back after work to take you home." If Zhu
begins to cry, describe what you perceive to be his feelings, *e.g.*,
"You are crying because you don't want Mom and Dad to go.
I'm going to be here with you."

WHY AM I DOING THIS?

Zhu and his parents need support and connection during this
transition time to help cope with their separation anxiety.
Giving this transition time and attention strengthens the trust
and attachment Zhu has with his parents and caregiver.
Caregivers who understand, acknowledge and assist with a
difficult separation create strong partnerships with parents
and their infants.

CONCEPTUAL FRAMEWORK:

Child's Point of View:

"I don't want you to go!"

Why Does This Matter?

Infants need physical and emotional support to cope with emotional distress. Physical and emotional support gives the message to the infant that his feelings are acknowledged and important. When the infant is reassured in moments of distress, his positive social and emotional growth is fostered.

COMMON BEHAVIOR AND NORMAL DEVELOPMENT:

Between seven and eleven months infants begin to understand that when their parents leave, they are no longer with them. We commonly refer to the consequently displayed sadness and fear as "separation anxiety."

ATTITUDES THAT CREATE
CARING COMMUNITIES:

✦ "When you are feeling emotional distress, I will help you cope with it."

SKILLS FOR CONSCIOUS
EVERYDAY RESPONSES:

✦ Acknowledging and describing an infant's separation anxiety and holding him / her validates that the emotions are real and important.

IF YOU NEED MORE:

Other conscious ways for the adult to stay objective and rational:

Continue holding and comforting Zhu as long as possible.

If other children and families arrive while Zhu is crying, the caregiver might say, **"Zhu is feeling sad this morning, so I am holding him."**

If he continues to cry and the caregiver must care for another child, keep Zhu as close as possible while you care for Sara. Say, **"Zhu, I am going to take care of Sara now, but you can sit here with us."**

Singing with Babies

Understanding Child Development

SITUATION:

Four infants, ages three to eight months, are gathered by the adults in the toy area of the infant room for singing. Johnny, four months old, is on the floor with several infant toys. Another adult brings Megan, eight months old, and Adam, six months old, to the group. The remaining infants are brought to the group from breakfast. The adults begin to sing "Eensy, Weensy Spider" with hand motions. As the adults sing, Megan begins to crawl away, Johnny reaches for a toy and puts it in his mouth, while Adam claps and rocks to the music.

COMMON ADULT RESPONSE:

An adult picks up Johnny and turns him around so he faces the group. She then retrieves Megan and puts her in her lap. The leader says, "You need to stay with us because we are singing now. Adam, you really liked that, didn't you? Do you want to sing another song?" The adult waits for his response. Adam keeps bouncing and smiling so the adult begins to sing another song.

CONSCIOUS ADULT RESPONSE:

Caring and Descriptive Language:

The adult is sitting on the floor and notices that Adam is not engaged in an activity. Knowing that Adam enjoyed "Eensy, Weensy Spider" yesterday, she begins to sing and do the hand motions to the song. Once the song is started, Adam crawls over to the singer. She says to him, **"You like this song, don't you?"** and sings it again with him. The adult observes that Adam is still enjoying it and says, **"Let's sing it again."**

While they are singing, Megan is crawling around the room. She crawls over to them, stops for a moment and crawls away.

Johnny, who is on the floor beside them, continues to mouth the toys that are around him.

WHY AM I DOING THIS?

The interests of the infant, *e.g.*, moving and exploring, mouthing objects in the environment and enjoying music, should be respected and not interrupted. The caring and conscious adult supports the infant's developing interest in music and does not force the infant to listen to music before he/she is interested.

CONCEPTUAL FRAMEWORK:

Child's Point of View:

For Adam: "I like the Eensy, Weensy Spider."

For Megan: "I need to move to explore."

For Johnny: "I need to mouth objects to explore."

Why Does This Matter?

Singing, like conversations, stimulates brain development and helps build relationships, but expecting infants to sit still is not appropriate. Infants are naturally attracted to music and rhythm and will clearly indicate their interest when ready.

COMMON BEHAVIOR AND NORMAL DEVELOPMENT:

Interrupting a child's focus and attention limits healthy development.

Immobile infants explore their environments by touching and mouthing objects within their grasp. The immobile infant is dependent on adults to provide a variety of appropriate toys and objects of a safe size within their reach.

When infants become mobile, they explore and internalize their environments by moving and touching. Freedom to move is essential for brain development.

Singing with children is appropriate and essential for language, social, and emotional development. It should happen spontaneously throughout the day:

✦ Sing songs with children's names in them or make up songs about what the children are doing

✦ Sing to comfort children in times of distress or to relax them

✦ Sing in response to infants' cooing and other vocalizations

✦ Respond to a variety of music in the environment, *e.g.*, cultural, classical, percussion

✦ Sing during diaper changing or dressing

✦ Sing songs that families sing at home

✦ Sing while changing from one activity to another

+ Sing favorite songs over and over again
+ Initiate singing in response to a lull in activity
+ "Dance" with infants that show interest in particular music or rhythm

Observing infants' responses to music and rhythm is the key to supporting them musically and planning other music experiences for those who are interested in them. Repetition enables children to internalize the language and structure of the song, which is the foundation for future reading and writing.

ATTITUDES THAT CREATE CARING COMMUNITIES:

+ "We will sing songs and listen to music throughout the day."

SKILLS FOR CONSCIOUS EVERYDAY RESPONSES:

+ Use music and rhythm spontaneously throughout the day.

IF YOU NEED MORE:

Other conscious ways for the adult to stay objective and rational:

If no infants respond to the song, try singing another familiar song.

If no infants respond, try singing again at another time.

Consider playing classical music in the background at times throughout the day, perhaps even very softly during nap times.

Chapter Two 2

Mobile Infants

Mobile infants are moving toward autonomy and independence through their newly found mobility. Curiosity drives their passion for exploration. Children who feel secure attachment with the adults in their environment will risk moving out and away from the adults to explore. Caring for mobile infants can be endearing, exciting and challenging. It takes great amounts of energy to keep up with and ahead of their movements and curiosity. To ensure the security and safety of mobile infants, adults need to be vigilant, aware, and knowledgeable in child development.

Healthy mobile infants:

+ Are competent and capable
+ Are persistent and single-minded
+ Are far more aware than their verbal ability might indicate
+ Are affectionate and social
+ Need secure, healthy relationships with adults
+ Need to move and explore
+ Are curious about the world around them
+ Are leery of separation and strangers
+ Respond physically to emotions
+ Have boundless energy
+ Are beginning to develop and control their fine and gross motor skills

What mobile infants need from adults:

+ Opportunity to develop independence
+ Safety and security with reasonable boundaries
+ Physical closeness
+ To feel loved unconditionally
+ To be able to move about with the adult
+ To see acceptable social behavior modeled
+ A sense of belonging
+ To hear spoken language

I Like Your Hair

Curiosity and Exploration

SITUATION:

Shanika, age 7 months, is sitting and watching Kevin, age 8 months, play with a ball. Shanika begins to crawl over to where Kevin is, reaches out, and touches his hair. She grasps some in her hand and pulls it towards her. Kevin begins to cry.

COMMON ADULT RESPONSE:

"Shanika, don't pull Kevin's hair!" The adult moves to release Shanika's hand from Kevin's hair and moves her away from Kevin.

Conscious Adult Response:

Caring and Descriptive Language:

The adult gets down on Kevin and Shanika's physical level.

For Shanika: The adult gently releases Shanika's hand from Kevin's hair and gently says, **"You were pulling Kevin's hair. That hurt him."**

For Kevin: The adult looks directly at Kevin and says, **"Kevin, when your hair is pulled, it hurts."** The adult looks at Kevin for his cues. **"Do you want me to pick you up?"** The adult puts her hands out so that if he wants to be held, he is able to make that choice. Kevin or Shanika may or may not climb into her arms.

For Shanika: Once Kevin is comforted, the adult opens Shanika's hand and rubs Shanika's open hand in a circular motion. The adult then takes Shanika's open hand and rubs it on her hair, saying, **"This is how my hair feels. Let's feel your hair."** She then has Shanika feel her own hair. The adult looks at Kevin to read his cues

and determine if he is open to Shanika's feeling his hair with the adult's assistance.

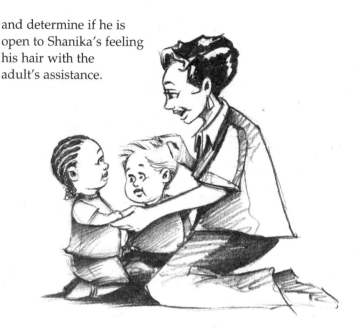

WHY AM I DOING THIS?

✦ The adult stopped the pulling and assisted Shanika in releasing the hair while describing Shanika's action and how it affected Kevin.

✦ The adult described what happened and how it felt and gave Kevin a choice about how he needed to be comforted.

✦ The adult modeled and assisted Shanika in feeling with an open hand and provided language for the action.

CONCEPTUAL FRAMEWORK:

Child's Point of View:

"I see your hair moving. It looks interesting and I want to touch it."

Why Does This Matter?

Children this age have mobility, and therefore become explorers following whatever piques their curiosity. Curiosity and exploration lead to social connections with other children that need to be understood and supported by the adults around them. Adults often interpret these initial attempts at socialization and active exploration as aggressive behaviors.

COMMON BEHAVIOR AND NORMAL DEVELOPMENT:

Mobile infants gain understanding of their world by exploring through their senses. Children still find a need to bring things to their mouth as a way to learn. They need to grab, hold and release objects. The hair, in this case, became the object that Shanika wanted to grab and hold and possibly bring to her mouth. Other children are seen as interesting, moving "objects" that stimulate curiosity and motivate exploration. Children of this age are fascinated with each other's hair. Feeling hair with an open hand models an acceptable way of touching others without hurting each other.

ATTITUDES THAT CREATE CARING COMMUNITIES:

✦ I will show you ways to explore and interact with other children without hurting them.

SKILLS FOR CONSCIOUS EVERYDAY RESPONSES:

✦ Show children ways to do things that don't hurt others

✦ Describe results of children's actions

✦ Support safe mobility and exploration

IF YOU NEED MORE:

Other conscious ways for the adult to stay objective and rational:

If Kevin can't be comforted quickly, give him the time he needs to calm down.

If Shanika persists in grabbing Kevin's hair, move her to another area of the room.

Shanika may become attracted to the action/reaction of touching/pulling hair. The adult may then "shadow" Shanika to watch, wait, and intervene if necessary to model feeling hair with an open hand.

The Truck Won't Go

Working Through Frustration

SITUATION:

Jamar, 10 months old, is just beginning to walk on his own. In
the play area, there is a large fire truck that children can ride
upon. Jamar crawls over to the fire truck, pulls himself up to
a standing position and starts to push it across the floor. He
pushes the fire truck into the wall. The truck stops. He starts
to scream and pushes the truck back and forth, banging it
into the wall.

COMMON ADULT RESPONSE:

"Jamar, don't push the truck into the wall." The caregiver picks him up, turns the truck around and sets him down behind it so he can continue to push the truck.

CONSCIOUS ADULT RESPONSE:

Caring and Descriptive Language:

"Jamar, you are pushing the truck and can't go any farther. You're upset because the wall is in the way. We can turn the truck around so you can push it some more." Stop a moment and watch how Jamar reacts to what you have said. He may

attempt to turn the truck around by himself. If he succeeds, say, **"You turned the truck around by yourself."** If assistance becomes necessary, verbally walk him through the process of turning the truck around.

Jamar may also turn, look at the caregiver and wait. If so, the caregiver says, **"Let's turn the truck around together."** The adult will have to turn the truck with Jamar often so he can learn to do it by himself.

WHY AM I DOING THIS?

Describing children's actions and allowing time for them to react often helps break the cycle of frustration.

Giving children choices, verbal assistance, time to practice and support allows them to feel capable enough to work out their own problems.

CONCEPTUAL FRAMEWORK:
Child's Point of View:

"I like pushing the truck, but the wall is in my way."

Why Does This Matter?

By pushing an object with wheels, mobile infants continue to develop their sense of independence and control through their new mobility. This may lead to their frustration with the objects or things that get in the way of their movement.

COMMON BEHAVIOR AND NORMAL DEVELOPMENT:

Children at this age need to move and push things around. Walking while pushing an object is a new skill for a child and frustration is a normal reaction if his or her movement is stopped, *e.g.*, running into the wall, having the truck tip over, wheels getting caught on the rug, etc. They don't have the language to identify their problem or ask for help in solving the problem.

It is important for adults to support and encourage this stage of development by:

+ Providing inside and outside space to practice

+ Providing equipment for this kind of movement

+ Providing language that describes the situation and the feelings that cause the frustration

+ Helping children work out the problem

ATTITUDES THAT CREATE CARING COMMUNITIES:

+ I will provide safe opportunities for you to practice your new skills. When you are confronted with frustrations, I will support you in solving the problem that caused your frustrations.

SKILLS FOR CONSCIOUS EVERYDAY RESPONSES:

✦ Describe the actions that create a problem

✦ Acknowledge frustrations and connect them to the problem that caused them

✦ Model problem solving

IF YOU NEED MORE:

Other conscious ways for the adult to stay objective and rational:

If Jamar continues to bang the truck into the wall and becomes increasingly frustrated, the caregiver can place a hand on the truck to physically stop it, saying, **"You are very angry with the wall, but banging the truck against the wall may break the truck. You have to stop."**

Put arms out in an inviting way and say, **"Why don't you come and sit down for a while?"**

If Jamar doesn't want to sit on the adult's lap and continues to bang the truck into the wall, the caregiver should take away the truck, saying, **"I am taking the truck away."** The caregiver then returns and sits beside Jamar, offering physical comfort and other activities.

I Want That Now!

Hitting, Biting and Their Physical Responses

SITUATION:

Bradley, age 12 months, is sitting on the floor playing with blocks. Molly, age 14 months, comes and takes the blocks from Bradley. Bradley screams and hits her. Molly starts to cry, too.

COMMON ADULT RESPONSE:

"Bradley, we don't hit. Molly, give that back to him."

Conscious Adult Response:

Caring and Descriptive Language:

The adult sits between the two children, physically comforting both of them. When the crying subsides, she/he might say to Bradley, **"Molly wanted the block. She took it and you hit her. Now she's crying. Hitting hurts."**

Turning to Molly: **"Molly, you wanted the block. When you took it, Bradley hit you. If you want the block, ask, 'May I have it, please?' Let's give it back and try asking."**

Support Molly giving the block back and her asking for it. She may just say, "Please?," which is appropriate.

Why Am I Doing This?

✦ The adult has supported both children by giving them language to express their actions and feelings.

✦ Even though Bradley may not completely understand what you are saying, the adult builds his foundation for language by describing Bradley's behavior and feelings. Adults should watch for these situations to prevent hitting and provide appropriate language. (By pointing out

Molly's tears to Bradley, the adult is describing a physical manifestation of the pain hitting can cause.)

✦ The focus in this scenario is not sharing, but using language to describe actions and acknowledge feelings.

CONCEPTUAL FRAMEWORK:

Child's Point of View:

For Molly: "I see you playing with the blocks. I want them."

For Bradley: "Don't take my blocks."

Why Does This Matter?

Children need to learn alternatives to hurting others to get their needs met. Modeling compassionate and caring conflict resolution lays the foundation for these children to experience how language is essential to problem solve. For example, when the blocks were taken away from Bradley, he did not have the language to express his feelings and/or needs, *e.g.*, "I'm playing with this now." By hitting, he says this non-verbally. He was hitting not to hurt her, but to express a feeling for which he lacked the correct language.

Children of this age have no awareness of how their actions impact others. For example, Molly sees the blocks "come alive" in the way Bradley is playing with them and wants to play with them. She, too, lacks the language to ask for them, so she takes them. When Bradley hit her, she could have hit him back, but instead she internalized the hurt or surprise and cried. She did not have the language to say, "You hurt me."

COMMON BEHAVIOR AND NORMAL DEVELOPMENT:

Physical responses are common behaviors when children do not have language to express their needs or feelings. Mobile infants are often interested in the toy being played with, even though there may be more of the same toy available in the classroom, because the toy being played with has movement and is therefore more interesting.

ATTITUDES THAT CREATE CARING COMMUNITIES:

+ "It is not OK to hurt someone. We will comfort anyone who is hurt."

SKILLS FOR CONSCIOUS EVERYDAY RESPONSES:

+ Describe what children do
+ Acknowledge their feelings
+ Comfort them
+ Show them alternative ways to meet their needs

IF YOU NEED MORE:

Other conscious ways for the adult to stay objective and rational:

If Bradley does not want to let her have the block, then say to Molly, **"Bradley still wants to play with it. Let's go find something else to play with."** Take her hand gently and walk toward the other materials. Stay with Molly until she is actively involved with other materials. By taking her hand, you are supporting her in finding something else with which to get involved.

Biting Hurts

Adult Intervention and Prevention

SITUATION:

Brittany, 18 months, and Jermaine, 16 months, are playing.
Brittany drops a toy she is carrying and walks away. Jermaine
picks up the toy and begins to play with it. Brittany returns to
find Jermaine playing with the doll. Brittany grabs the toy.
When met with resistance, she leans over and bites Jermaine's
hand. Jermaine screams while still holding onto the toy.

COMMON ADULT RESPONSE:

"Brittany! We bite food, not our friends. Give Jermaine the toy."

CONSCIOUS ADULT RESPONSE:

Caring and Descriptive Language:

The adult moves quickly to get physically close to both children. Focusing on Jermaine, the adult says, **"Jermaine, that bite hurt, didn't it?"** (Pause) **"There is a problem. Brittany grabbed the toy from you and bit you. Brittany wanted the toy. When you didn't give it back, she bit you. The bite hurt a lot.**

"Look, Brittany, he's crying. When you bite him, it hurts him.
Look at Jermaine's hand. Your teeth made those marks on his
hand." The caregiver gently rubs Jermaine's hand.

After Jermaine has been comforted, the caregiver turns to
Brittany and say, **"Brittany, I know you had the toy before
Jermaine did, but you put it down and walked away. When
you saw Jermaine pick it up, you wanted it back, so you
grabbed it. When he didn't give it to you, you bit him. Biting
hurts people. You cannot bite when you want the toy. What
you can do is walk to Jermaine, hold out your hands, and say,
'Please, may I have the toy?' Will you try that for me?"**
(Brittany will respond with whatever language she can. In this
case, she might respond by repeating, "Please, toy?")

If Jermaine gives her the toy, describe what happened. **"You
asked him for the toy, and he gave it to you."**

If Jermaine refuses to give her the toy, the adult describes what
happened. **"Jermaine does not want to give you the toy now.
Let's go find another toy for you to play with."** The adult
stays with Brittany until she is engaged.

WHY AM I DOING THIS?

+ Providing specific descriptions of what children do gives
  language and meaning to their actions. Focusing on the
  biting and the bite mark helps Brittany become more
  aware of her behavior and its consequences. Pausing after
  a question or a statement gives the child an opportunity
  to focus on what was said and respond. It may also serve
  as a pause in the emotional reactions taking place. Gentle
  rubbing of the hurt models an empathetic response.

+ The adult stated clearly that Brittany should not bite because
  it hurts. She then offered her a specific alternative to get the
  toy. We have given Brittany language she can use. Jermaine
  was given a choice to give up the doll or not. The adult

supported Brittany until she was actively engaged elsewhere so the conflict wouldn't reoccur.

✦ The adult must be vigilant in watching or shadowing Brittany in order to prevent it from happening again. If the adult perceives that Brittany is about to bite again, he or she must prevent the biting by, *e.g.*, taking her by the hand, picking her up, turning her body away from the other child, placing a hand between her and the other child, or placing his/her body between the two children.

These strategies are nonverbal adult responses to prevent the danger of biting. These strategies do not verbally focus on biting because no biting has taken place yet, and Brittany should not get attention for biting.

CONCEPTUAL FRAMEWORK:

Child's Point of View:

"I played with that toy, so it's mine, even though I put it down. When you wouldn't give it back to me, I had to bite you to get it back."

Why Does This Matter?

Mobile infants create personal strategies to get their needs met. In this case, it was biting, which is painful and dangerous.

COMMON BEHAVIOR AND NORMAL DEVELOPMENT:

At this age, children are very possessive of items. They believe that what they see and touch is theirs. This often results in conflict. Biting, which usually begins when children are about one and one-half years old, is a common response.

Adults must be vigilant and ready to step in quickly in a firm and caring manner to prevent the biting. In some cases, having something for the child to bite, *e.g.*, a teether attached to the child's clothing, satisfies the urge to bite. Once a child has bitten, the adult must stay close by the child and closely follow his / her actions so that the biting, which happens quickly, does not recur. With conscious adult responses, the biting will decrease, and yet occasional biting may occur despite vigilant efforts. This is a very difficult stage of development that demands constant adult awareness.

ATTITUDES THAT CREATE
CARING COMMUNITIES:

✦ "Everyone must feel safe here. I will show you ways to ask for what you want that do not hurt anyone."

SKILLS FOR CONSCIOUS
EVERYDAY RESPONSES:

✦ Watch for situations involving ownership and possession issues

✦ Prevent danger through nonverbal interventions and redirections

✦ Provide language and model empathy when someone is hurt

✦ Give time and caring commitment to the problem-solving process

IF YOU NEED MORE:

Other conscious ways for the adult to stay objective and rational:

If Brittany cannot accept Jermaine's "no," acknowledge her feelings. **"Brittany, I can see that you are unhappy because Jermaine wants to keep the toy. I will help you find something else to play with."**

Continuity of Care

Emotional and Physical Transitions

SITUATION:

Loraina is 15 months old and has been walking for three months. The caregivers notice that her activity level has increased, and she now takes only one nap a day. Her family and teachers decide that it is time to begin her transition to the toddler room. The childcare center's policy is that the child visits the toddler room with a familiar caregiver for an increasingly longer period each day for a week. During this first week, Loraina cries continuously.

COMMON ADULT RESPONSE:

"I can't stay here with you, Loraina. You'll just have to get used to this room."

CONSCIOUS ADULT RESPONSE:

Caring and Descriptive Language:

The caregiver realizes that Loraina is not adapting to the new environment and knows that the best thing for her is the environment and adults with which she is familiar. She first talks to her coworkers in the infant room about this. Upon gaining their support, she speaks with the center's director about keeping Loraina in the room and modifying the environment to meet Loraina's needs as a toddler.

"I have been learning about continuity of care. The caregivers stay with the same children for three years. I never thought about our transition policy before, but after seeing Loraina in such emotional distress, I would like to try it. My coworkers think it's a good idea, too." The caregiver and director discuss logistics for the long-range continuity of care plan. After doing so, they invite in Loraina's parents to talk about the plan.

WHY AM I DOING THIS?

The caregiver has acknowledged Loraina's distress at leaving her familiar environment and realizes that she does not want Loraina to leave her, either. Adults and infants create strong attachments. Breaking these strong bonds is not healthy for either the adult or child in the first years of life. This caregiver has recognized a better way to support the development of trust, security and attachment through continuity of care. She has the support of coworkers and the director to explore and develop this new practice. By keeping Loraina in the same environment, she will be able to support her physical and intellectual development while adapting this environment to meet her changing needs.

CONCEPTUAL FRAMEWORK:

Child's Point of View:

"I don't want you to leave me."

"I am afraid of this unfamiliar place."

Why Does This Matter?

When children exhibit behaviors of stress, *e.g.*, crying and clinging, they should be taken seriously. The child's fears may seem unfounded since the adult knows that all of the rooms within the center are a safe environment. However, the child is experiencing real fear. His or her feelings must not be discounted; instead, these feelings must be acknowledged and supported as we help the child work through them.

Continuity of care relieves the stress of breaking the bond with familiar caregivers and entering an unfamiliar environment at a very young age. Moving infants into new rooms when they become mobile and again when they become toddlers is not a best practice. The fewer the transitions, the better. Continuity of care eliminates multiple transitions in the early years.

COMMON BEHAVIOR AND NORMAL DEVELOPMENT:

Physical responses are common behaviors for mobile infants because they don't have the language to express their needs and feelings. Anxiety about separation from familiar people and environments is a normal response for many mobile infants and they often cry and cling to express their fear. If their needs for comfort and security are met through continuity of care, the emotional distress brought about by change is minimized during these first years.

Staying with the same caregivers for three years enables the child to develop trust in the familiar adults and environment. Adjusting the environment to meet the toddler's needs supports language, social and intellectual development.

ATTITUDES THAT CREATE CARING COMMUNITIES:

✦ "I will protect and nurture the attachment that we have created."

SKILLS FOR CONSCIOUS EVERYDAY RESPONSES:

✦ Comfort children physically and verbally when they need comforting

✦ Change the environment to meet developmental needs

IF YOU NEED MORE:

Other conscious ways for the adult to stay objective and rational:

If suggestions to create continuity of care meet resistance, tactfully enlist support from administrators or co-workers and early childhood teachers. Use professional articles as support.

You Fell on Me!

Physical Control and Motor Skills

SITUATION:

Ming and Ramon, both age 16 months, are on the playground.
Ramon kicks the big, green ball, and he and Ming both start
to chase it. The ball hits the fence and stops. Ming and Ramon
crash into the ball and they fall on top of one another. Both
children begin to cry.

COMMON ADULT RESPONSE:

"Be careful, don't hurt each other."

CONSCIOUS ADULT RESPONSE:

Caring and Descriptive Language:

"You were both running after the ball and couldn't stop. You fell on each other and it hurt." The adult sits on the ground with the children and asks both, "You are both crying. Crying means that you are hurt. Ramon, show me where it hurts. Ming, where does it hurt?" Acknowledge what the children do or say.

When the children have calmed down, say, "It's hard to stop when we are running. If something is in front of us, we have to stop or we will run into it and get hurt — just like what happened with the big, green ball. Do you want to chase the ball some more or roll it to each other?"

WHY AM I DOING THIS?

Describing children's actions and the consequences of their actions helps children become conscious of what they are doing. It also helps them understand what they are feeling. By asking where it hurt, the teacher is inviting the children to become involved in their own comforting.

The adult has described an action that the child has not yet refined, which is stopping, and acknowledged it and the consequences. Choices have been offered so children can reengage in an activity.

CONCEPTUAL FRAMEWORK:

Child's Point of View:

"I want to run after the ball."

Why Does This Matter?

Mobile infants need to move. Children need to be able to move so they can begin to control their movements.

The children are developing their sense of autonomy as they begin to move away physically and emotionally from the adult.

COMMON BEHAVIOR AND NORMAL DEVELOPMENT:

Running is a developmental skill. Once children can run, they often run into things and each other.

Children are beginning to create play situations that are independent from the adult.

ATTITUDES THAT CREATE CARING COMMUNITIES:

✦ I will support your need for movement and your emerging independence without compromising safety.

SKILLS FOR CONSCIOUS EVERYDAY RESPONSES:

- ✦ Know the stages of gross motor development
- ✦ Be conscious of safety issues
- ✦ Provide opportunities for children to move and play independently

IF YOU NEED MORE:

Other conscious ways for the adult to stay objective and rational:

If the adult can't comfort both children, call over another adult to help with one child.

If one child becomes angry at the other and attempts to hit or bite, the adult needs to intervene to stop it, then say, "**Ming, when you both fell down, you both got hurt. Ramon did not mean to hurt you. Look, he is crying too.**"

If children continue to chase the ball and fall down and hurt themselves, the adult will have to get directly involved in the play to ensure safety.

Chapter Three 3

Toddlers are developing their identity and are becoming more actively involved in their daily routines. Their increasing independence and insistence upon doing things for themselves make caring for and living with toddlers unpredictable, challenging and exciting. Adults need to hone their skills in reading cues and signals to determine when to stand firm and when to offer choices and flexibility. Adults should do their best to maintain a sense of humor and enjoy the wonder of toddlers' unfolding competence.

Healthy toddlers:

+ Have a strong sense of territory and possession
+ Have a strong need for physical connection with familiar adults, but an equally strong need to be physically independent from adults
+ Take things apart, empty things out and move from activity to activity to learn about their environment and their relationship to it
+ Have an emerging sense of curiosity about the people and situations in their environment
+ Begin to form friendships and partnerships in play situations
+ Express their emotions physically
+ Sense of independence often leads to resistive behavior, *e.g.*, "No!"
+ Enjoy music and movement

What Toddlers Need from Adults:

+ A sense of adventure, humor and unconditional love
+ Boundaries that allow them to make meaningful choices safely
+ Appropriate expectations based on knowledge and an understanding of their developmental needs and their behavior
+ Patience and the ability to observe before reacting
+ Time and space to create their own games and to interact with materials and people
+ Explanations and descriptions of what is going on in their world
+ The opportunity to learn and use language through conversation, stories, songs and play
+ A partner in their play and the routines of their daily lives

Toilet Learning

Understanding Readiness

SITUATION:

Barbara arrives at her mother Carol's house to pick up David, 30 months old, who spent the night there. Carol says to her daughter, "Barbara, I think it's long past time for David to be toilet trained. I had you toilet trained before you were two."

Barbara responds, "I can understand how you feel, Mom, and when I was looking for childcare, some of the centers I interviewed would not take David because he wasn't trained. However, the reason I chose to enroll him at the childcare center he attends is because they wait until he is ready. And I'm sorry, Mom, but he just isn't ready yet."

COMMON ADULT RESPONSE:

"Oh, nonsense. In my day, we decided when the child was ready and it worked out just fine," Carol says. "How are you suppose to know when David is ready?"

Barbara responds angrily, "That was 25 years ago, Mom. A lot has changed since then. Just let me worry about this, okay?"

CONSCIOUS ADULT RESPONSE:

Caring and Descriptive Language:

Instead of this becoming a heated, emotional argument based on their differing philosophies and experiences, Barbara explains to her mother her philosophy of toilet learning.

"Mom, I can see we have different ideas about how children learn to go to the bathroom by themselves. I have read a lot about this and have talked to David's caregivers. What I have learned is that children will let you know when they are ready to be toilet trained. Some of the signs are children staying dry longer and showing an interest in the toilet and

in others' using it. Children will often get a different look on their face when they are ready to urinate or have a bowel movement, or they tell you they want to use the toilet. David's teachers and I are waiting for these signs before we begin the process. Once these signs occur, we will train David and then put him in disposable pull-up diapers. That's what I think. Why do you think I should be doing it now?"

Carol replies, "Well, for one thing, we didn't have disposable diapers. We used cloth diapers. Once the cloth diapers got wet, I had to change you right away or you would get a diaper rash. You complained when your diapers were wet, so that motivated me to get you out of them. I notice David doesn't mind wearing a wet disposable diaper; I guess he doesn't feel wet or get diaper rashes. You liked wearing training panties. Maybe David would like wearing training pants, too, even though he is not ready."

Barbara says, "I wonder if David would like to wear disposable pull-up diapers?"

Carol replies, "Yes, he probably would. But when he is ready, I think he should wear training pants instead. That way, he can feel when he is wet."

WHY AM I DOING THIS?

Independent toileting is a *learning* process, not a *training* process.

Toilet learning can be a very emotional issue. By discussing different philosophies calmly and trying to understand other points of view, adults are more likely to reach an agreement about the child's toilet learning strategy.

Adults involved in a child's daily life need a clear understanding of the decided-upon toilet learning strategy and agree to abide by it.

CONCEPTUAL FRAMEWORK:

Child's Point of View:

"I need you to agree upon how and when I learn to go to the bathroom by myself."

Why Does This Matter?

Children need time, attention and collaboration from the adults in their lives to learn the process of independent toileting. This process varies according to the child's temperament, physical awareness and relationship to the adult.

COMMON BEHAVIOR AND NORMAL DEVELOPMENT

Adults must remember that not all children are ready for the same things at the same time. Toilet learning is influenced by culture, economics, age differences among adults, adults' self image and views regarding independence and dependence. As a result of these influences, it can be highly emotional and can have more to do with adults' issues than children's (*e.g.*, diapers expenses, a fear of failure, etc.).

Accidents may be common during this learning process.
Accidents should not be interpreted as a sign of defiance,
but rather as the result of a lapse in concentration, sleeping
soundly, etc. If the toilet learning process becomes
argumentative and difficult, it is not working. The adult
needs to assess the readiness of the child versus his or her
own desire for success. An adult who puts too much emphasis
on toilet learning may be more likely to respond harshly or
even abusively to accidents.

For children to learn independent toileting, they must be aware
of the sensation of elimination, develop control over stopping
and starting it, and know what to do when it occurs. They
must also want to do it. Toilet learning will occur when the
adult patiently supports the child throughout the time it takes
him or her to master the skill.

The physical discomfort of wet or soiled pants provides part
of the motivation to learn to go to the bathroom. Absorbent
disposable pull-up diapers keep the wetness away from the
toddlers skin until the diaper is totally saturated. As a result,

the child will rarely feel wet, which may discourage him or her from wanting to learn to go to the bathroom independently.

Dialogue about beliefs and practices regarding toilet learning creates awareness and will guide decisions and compromises made on behalf of a child's toilet learning.

ATTITUDES THAT CREATE CARING COMMUNITIES:

✦ I will work collaboratively with the other adults involved in your toilet learning.

SKILLS FOR CONSCIOUS EVERYDAY RESPONSES:

✦ Know the signs of readiness for independent toileting

✦ Plan a toilet learning strategy with the other significant adults in the child's life to ensure consistency

✦ Be patient and supportive in this learning process

IF YOU NEED MORE:

Other conscious ways for the adult to stay objective and rational:

Seek information, guidance, and support from your child's medical professional, family and friends, parenting magazines and books, and websites.

It's Circle Time

Realistic Expectations

SITUATION:

Kelly, 18 months old, Aaron, 16 months old, and Tyrone, 20 months old, are in a toddler classroom. This class has 12 children. According to the schedule, it is "circle time." All children are gathered onto the rug to form a circle. One adult begins to play guitar and sing a song. The children are attentive, either singing, clapping, or watching the adults. During the second song, Kelly stands and begins to dance. The other adult says, "Kelly, we sit at circle time," and gently sets Kelly back down. Aaron stands up and walks to the block area. She quickly gets up, carries Aaron back to the circle and says, "Circle time is not over. You need to sit with us, Aaron." Tyrone climbs into the lap of the teacher who is singing. He stops singing and says, "Tyrone, it's circle time, not hugging time." By the last song, the

children have been in the
circle for 20 minutes
and half of them
begin to wander off.
The other adult
herds them back
to the circle.

COMMON ADULT RESPONSE:

"Circle time is not over. You have to come back. When we are finished, you can play."

CONSCIOUS ADULT RESPONSE:

Caring and Descriptive Language:

Circle time for toddlers needs flexibility. The singing adult says to the other adult, **"I'm going to sing 'The Friends Song.' Let's see if the children are interested. I will stay with the children who want to sing and dance. You can be with the other children."** The adult gets his guitar, sits on the rug and starts to sing. Four or five children come to the rug and sit with him.

For Kelly: **"Kelly wants to dance to this song. She is standing and moving. Does anyone else want to stand up and dance?"**

For Aaron: The non-singing adult watching Aaron says, **"Aaron, I see you are finished singing and want to play with the blocks."**

For Tyrone: The singing teacher does not stop singing when Tyrone climbs into his lap. He continues to sing with him in his lap. After singing, the teacher says, **"Tyrone, you climbed into my lap quietly so we could all keep singing."**

WHY AM I DOING THIS?

✦ By communicating to the other adult what is going to happen, the needs of the children are met and the children are given choices.

✦ By describing and acknowledging what Kelly is doing, and inviting other children to follow her lead, the adult validates her idea.

✦ By respecting Aaron's choice to leave circle time and describing his choice to play in the block area, the adult respects his change of interest.

✦ By holding Tyrone and later describing his actions and acknowledging that he did not interrupt the activity, the adult fulfills Tyrone's need for physical closeness without interrupting the group's activity.

CONCEPTUAL FRAMEWORK:

Child's Point of View:

For Kelly: "I need to move to the music."

For Aaron: "I want to play with the blocks, not sit and sing."

For Tyrone: "I want to sit on your lap."

Why Does This Matter?

Extensive structured circle time is an unrealistic expectation of the adults. It does not support toddlers' developmental needs.

COMMON BEHAVIOR AND NORMAL DEVELOPMENT:

Toddlers will come together as a group, but then move out of the group and wander from one thing to another. This is the normal way for them to explore and make sense of their world. The more they move, the more they learn. A schedule that allows them to move in and out of all activities supports their learning process. Toddlers also learn by "onlooking," *i.e.*, not being directly involved in an activity, but aware and watching from afar.

Toddlers have a natural physical response to music. They are beginning to develop their sense of rhythm, beat, and melody, so they need to hear a wide variety of music and have many opportunities for movement to support this development.

Wanting physical connection with adults is a need for all toddlers. They communicate very clearly when they need this connection and when they do not. Responding to the children's signals is the adult's role in their relationship with the toddler.

Caring for toddlers in group care takes special planning and consideration. Being in a "group" for any length of time can be difficult for many toddlers. Providing opportunities for toddlers to become comfortable with group activities at their own pace and in their own time is critical in appropriate care. However, many activities, such as singing, dancing and reading, are spontaneous activities that happen throughout the day. Observations of spontaneous activities, such as singing and dancing, provide the basis for planning group activities that become more meaningful and increase involvement and interest.

Attitudes That Create Caring Communities:

✦ "I will not expect you to do things that are inappropriate for your age and stage of development."

Skills for Conscious Everyday Responses:

✦ Plan flexible group activities for toddlers

✦ Use music, movement and stories throughout the day

✦ Provide opportunities for physical connection between children and adults throughout the day

If You Need More:

Other conscious ways for the adult to stay objective and rational:

If a scheduled circle time is required by a program and children are not engaged in the activity:

✦ Implement multiple, short "circle" times, *e.g.*, three or four three-minute gatherings throughout the day

✦ Give children an opportunity to suggest songs they want to sing when appropriate.

Learning to Use Words

Setting an Example for Toddlers' Language

SITUATION:

Patrick is 28 months old. According to his mother, he has bitten his four-year-old brother twice during the week. Patrick is sitting in the adult's lap at the childcare center, reading a favorite book. Latoya, 35 months old, walks over with her favorite book. When Latoya reaches up toward the adult, Patrick turns and bites her hand. Latoya cries.

COMMON ADULT RESPONSE:

"Patrick, don't bite. You need to use your words. Say you are sorry."

CONSCIOUS ADULT RESPONSE:

Caring and Descriptive Language:

The adult puts Patrick on the floor beside her. The adult takes Latoya in her arms and comforts her, making sure there is a safe distance between the two children. At the same time, the adult looks at Patrick and says calmly, **"Patrick, you bit Latoya on the hand. It hurt her. She is crying."** Pause.

Looking at Latoya, the adult says, **"Latoya, Patrick bit your hand. That hurts a lot."** Describe the consequence of his action to both children.

The adult gently rubs Latoya's hand and says, **"Patrick, when someone is hurt, we help that person. I am gently rubbing Latoya's hand where you bit her. I hope it helps her feel better.**

Patrick, can you think of something to help Latoya feel better?" Acknowledge whatever Patrick says and Latoya will accept. If he doesn't reply, leave it for now.

"Patrick, you may never bite anyone. If Latoya sits too close to you, say, 'Latoya, you are too close, please move back.' When I am reading a story to you and you are sitting on my lap, you will stay on my lap and we will keep reading your story, even if someone else comes and sits down next to us." Before the adult resumes reading the story, with Patrick on her lap and Latoya beside her, she says. **"I am reading a story to Patrick now. You can listen with us."**

WHY AM I DOING THIS?

✦ The victim should always be comforted first when addressing this situation.

✦ By offering Patrick the opportunity to make empathetic responses, the adult creates the foundation for empathy, whether he chooses to respond at this time or not.

✦ By giving Patrick the exact words to use and respecting the activity they are doing together, the adult reassures him that another child cannot interrupt their activity.

CONCEPTUAL FRAMEWORK:

Child's Point of View:

"I don't want you to sit close to me."

"I'm sitting on her lap now and she is reading my story."

Why Does This Matter?

Children at this age, even though they have language, still react impulsively in emotional situations. They must hear and have problem-solving language modeled many times before they understand how to use it.

COMMON BEHAVIOR
AND NORMAL DEVELOPMENT:

Toddlers are possessive and territorial. These traits are very intense and emotional. It is unrealistic for adults to expect a toddler who is having an intense emotional reaction to stop, think, and "use their words," or to know these words after they have been modeled only once or twice. The expectation for independent use of problem-solving language is appropriate for much older children. However, it is realistic for the adult to use "the words" with and for the children as each problem arises.

Toddlers don't like to be crowded. They are beginning to define their own personal space. If they feel crowded, they will react. On the other hand, they do not have a consciousness of another person's personal space.

Biting episodes may occur or recur, even though toddlers are becoming more verbal. It may be an emotional response triggered by a change in their life, *e.g.*, a new baby, moving to a new home, etc., which takes over and prevents them from accessing language they may have.

ATTITUDES THAT CREATE CARING COMMUNITIES:

✦ "I will not let you hurt anyone. I will give you 'the words' to ask for what you want and express what you feel."

SKILLS FOR CONSCIOUS EVERYDAY RESPONSES:

✦ Model empathy with words and actions

✦ Use problem-solving language

✦ Respect time and space together

IF YOU NEED MORE:

Other conscious ways for the adult to stay objective and rational:

If Patrick continues to try to bite or continues to be upset because Latoya is near them, stop reading the story and say, **"Let's sit here together until you feel calm. Then we can read your story again, Patrick."**

No!

Resistive Behavior and the Need for Independence

SITUATION:

Orlando, 24 months old, is sitting at a table having a snack. As he drinks his milk, he spills it all over the table and his shirt. The adult says, "Orlando, you spilled the milk on your shirt. We need to get you a dry one. Let's go change your shirt." He goes with the adult to get changed, and she removes his shirt. As she turns to get him a clean one, Orlando runs back to the table. As the adult goes to the table with the shirt, Orlando looks at her, says "No!" and runs away laughing. When the adult catches up to him, Orlando says "No!" again and tries to squirm away.

COMMON ADULT RESPONSE:

"Orlando, stop squirming. We are putting on your shirt now."

CONSCIOUS ADULT RESPONSE:

Caring and Descriptive Language:

"Orlando, you like running away and having me chase you. That's like a game, isn't it?"

If the weather is appropriate for Orlando to be without his shirt for a few minutes: "Orlando, do you like having your shirt off?" Pause. "Here is your clean shirt. I will leave it on this chair. You can put it on now, or you can put it on when you are ready. If you need my help, let me know." Support whichever choice he makes.

If the weather is not appropriate: "Orlando, do you like having your shirt off?" Pause. "It's cold today, so you have to wear a shirt. Do you want to put it on by yourself, or do you want me to help you?" Support whichever choice he makes.

WHY AM I DOING THIS?

✦ Describing the child's behavior helps defuse any annoyance the adult may feel in response to the resistive behavior.

✦ Making the choice of when to put the shirt on supports the child's need for independence. This response may be appropriate depending upon weather and circumstances. Even if weather and circumstances do not permit Orlando to be without a shirt, a choice is still offered.

CONCEPTUAL FRAMEWORK:
Child's Point of View:

"I don't want to put my shirt on for you right now."

Why Does This Matter?

Becoming independent is built on making many small decisions. Toddlers need to make decisions on how and when to assert their independence. The adult must support their decision-making based on assessing the appropriateness and safety of the situation, the child's skill levels, and time and schedules.

COMMON BEHAVIOR AND NORMAL DEVELOPMENT:

The process of becoming independent is a primary job of toddlers. They do it by physically and verbally separating themselves from the adult. Their language is developing, enabling them to state their needs. "No" and "Me do it" are two common phrases toddlers use to state their need for independence. While this can be a frustrating experience for the adult, it is a necessary stage of development for the toddler.

Toddlers are beginning to realize they are a separate entity from the adult. This leads them into more independent activities, *e.g.*, putting on their own shirt. At the same time, they need to know the adult is there for them when they need him/her.

"Running away" is another way that toddlers assert their independence — usually with great joy! They are seeking a partner in the game they are creating: "I'm running away, so you chase me." When toddlers do this, they aren't pushing the adult away. Rather, they are seeking engagement with the adult on their terms. With this knowledge, adults can become willing partners in this developmental game.

Part of a toddler's self-awareness is becoming conscious of their physical body. The air on their skin is a physical sensation that many toddlers find pleasant, so they like it when they take off their clothes.

ATTITUDES THAT CREATE CARING COMMUNITIES:

✦ "When you assert your independence, I will provide limits that will keep you safe and give you appropriate choices."

SKILLS FOR CONSCIOUS EVERYDAY RESPONSES:

✦ Provide opportunities for children to make choices in order to develop their independence

✦ Successful relationships with toddlers depend on the adult's knowing when the situation calls for flexibility.

IF YOU NEED MORE:

Other conscious ways for the adult to stay objective and rational:

If the adult has determined that Orlando must wear his shirt, but he refuses to put it on (*e.g.*, continues to say "No!", runs away, or tries to wiggle away), the adult says, **"Orlando, I know you don't want to wear a shirt, but it's time to put on your shirt now. I am putting it over your head. Can you help me pull it down? Let's put this arm in first. Can you push it through? Can you do the other arm by yourself?"** Bringing attention to the process of putting on his shirt may lessen his resistance, which may make him a "partner" in the process. He may maintain his resistance and make putting on his shirt a "wrestling match." In either case, the process of putting on the shirt and describing what is being done continues. When the shirt is on, the adult acknowledges, **"Orlando, I know you did not want to put on the shirt."** Read the child's cues to determine if he needs comfort from the situation or if he needs time alone.

Big Boys and Girls Don't Cry

Misinterpreting Children's Behavior and Intentions

SITUATION:

Kendrick, age 30 months, is by himself playing with blocks. He begins to cry. A male caregiver stands over him with his hands on his hips.

Rosa, age 27 months, returns after a week's illness. She cries and asks for her mother throughout the day. When Rosa's mother arrives at the door, Rosa runs to her. The caregiver describes Rosa's crying to her mother and says, "Rosa cried all day and I have other children to take care of."

COMMON ADULT RESPONSE:

"Kendrick, why are you being such a crybaby today? I know you're not a baby. Do you want me to hold you like a baby?"

"Rosa, you cried a lot today, but I know you are not going to cry like that tomorrow, are you?"

CONSCIOUS ADULT RESPONSE:

Caring and Descriptive Language:

For Kendrick: The caregiver gets down on the floor next to Kendrick and says softly, **"Kendrick, you're crying. You seem sad. Would you like for me to hold you?"** The caregiver holds out his arms, inviting Kendrick to climb onto his lap. The caregiver sits with Kendrick as long as he needs to cry.

For Rosa: Each time Rosa cries during the day, her caregiver goes to her and sits down beside her, offering her lap with outstretched hands. She says in a quiet, caring manner, **"You have not been here for a while because you were sick. I am so glad you are back. I missed you when you weren't here."** Pause. If she continues to cry, say, **"You are crying because you want your mom."** At some point during the day, acknowledge Rosa's discomfort to the group and ask if they can help their friend. Remind her, **"Remember, when you wake up from your nap, your mom will come to take you home."**

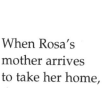

When Rosa's mother arrives to take her home, the caregiver acknowledges Rosa's difficult day. **"Since Rosa was home with you for a week, she cried a lot today. This is normal after an absence. I comforted her and reassured her that you would pick her up after her nap. In the morning when you drop her off, you might also want to tell her that you will pick her up after her nap."**

To Rosa, say, **"If you still miss your mom tomorrow and need to cry, you can come and sit in my lap."**

WHY AM I DOING THIS?

✦ By sitting next to Kendrick on the floor and observing and describing Kendrick's behavior, *e.g.*, crying softly, the caregiver gives physical support and helps Kendrick connect his crying to sadness. Holding Kendrick also provides him with an opportunity to talk about his sadness.

✦ By sitting beside the child and offering a lap to sit on, the caregiver offers physical comfort. By acknowledging and describing Rosa's absence and Rosa's need for her mother, the caregiver offers reassurance. The caregiver also offers reassurance by describing her own feelings about Rosa.

✦ By describing Rosa's day in an objective, caring way to her mom, the caregiver reassures Rosa that she will be supported emotionally the next day if needed and gives the mother language to support Rosa at home.

CONCEPTUAL FRAMEWORK:
Child's Point of View:

Kendrick: "I am feeling sad."

Rosa: "I don't feel well, and I want to be home with my mom."

Why Does This Matter?

Crying is an expression of the child's feelings. Conscious acknowledgement assures children that their feelings are valid and respected. If the adult responds to crying in an understanding and compassionate manner, the child's positive self-image can be strengthened. If the response to crying is sarcastic or condescending, the child's self image can be weakened.

COMMON BEHAVIOR AND NORMAL DEVELOPMENT:

Children have strong feelings that they express physically. Crying expresses physical or emotional pain. They are not yet able to connect their behavior to their feelings. They are overtaken by an emotion and react to it without understanding why. By continually describing behavior and making connections between the behavior and what the child seems to be feeling, the adult validates the behavior. This validation provides a message to the child: "My feelings matter and I will be supported while I try to cope." This also provides a message to the adult: "The child's feelings are very real."

ATTITUDES THAT CREATE CARING COMMUNITIES:

✦ "If you need to cry, I will provide physical comfort, emotional support, and caring, descriptive language to help you understand and cope."

SKILLS FOR CONSCIOUS EVERYDAY RESPONSES:

✦ Acknowledge that children's feelings are real

✦ Let the children know that crying is a healthy and appropriate expression of pain, fear, hurt, etc.

✦ Model and support coping behaviors

IF YOU NEED MORE:

Other conscious ways for the adult to stay objective and rational:

For Kendrick: If he cannot be consoled, ask questions to rule out physical discomfort, *e.g.*, "**Kendrick, what is hurting you?**"

For Rosa: If Rosa cannot be consoled, call Rosa's mother (if possible) so Rosa can talk to her for reassurance. The mother can determine whether she wants to pick up Rosa early.

If she can't be consoled and the caregiver has to attend to other activities, he or she might say, "**Rosa, I know that you are very upset, but I need to get lunch ready. You can sit here so you can see me while I prepare lunch, or you can stay and play.**" The caregiver should support Rosa's decision, but be sure to begin the next activity promptly to keep the group's schedule on track.

For Kendrick and Rosa: If children cannot be consoled or comforted, they can be left alone in some cases, but should be kept in sight by the adult: "**Maybe you would like to be alone now?**" If they appear to be tired, provide an opportunity for them to sleep.

It's Mine!

A Toddler's Sense of Possession

SITUATION:

Marie, 32 months old, walks over to Carrie, 18 months old, who is pushing a stroller. Marie says "It's mine," and takes it away from her. Carrie turns to get a teddy bear. Marie takes the bear away and says, "It's mine." Carrie wanders across the room and finds a pull toy. Marie watches, takes the toy away from her and again says, "It's mine."

COMMON ADULT RESPONSE:

"Marie, stop taking things away from Carrie." The adult takes the doggie pull toy away from Marie and gives it back to Carrie. "You need to share. Here, you play with this toy." The adult hands Marie another toy.

CONSCIOUS ADULT RESPONSE:

Caring and Descriptive Language:

When the adult sees Marie take the doggie pull toy away from Carrie, he/she gets down on the children's level, with Carrie on one side and Marie on the other, and says, **"Marie, Carrie is pulling the doggie toy now. If you want it, you have to ask her. Say, 'Carrie, may I please have the doggie?'"** Give Marie the opportunity to say the words, then turn to Carrie and say, **"Marie has asked you if she can play with the doggie. You are playing with it now. Do you want to give it to her?"**

If Carrie says or indicates "yes," say, **"Marie, Carrie is giving you the doggie. Say, 'Thank you for giving me the doggie.'"**

If Carrie says or indicates "no," say, **"Marie, Carrie does not want to give you the doggie now. She is playing with it, so it is hers for now. I will help you find something else to play with."** When Marie finds something to play with, say, **"Marie, you are playing with the doll. It's yours for now."** (You will probably have to do this many times.)

WHY AM I DOING THIS?

✦ Describing who has the toy at the moment gives meaning, language and boundaries to ownership and possession.

✦ Allowing Carrie to decide whether or not she gives up the toy acknowledges that she has possession and she alone decides whether or not she keeps it. Adult presence is essential in facilitating Carrie's choices.

CONCEPTUAL FRAMEWORK:

Child's Point of View:

"I see it, it is mine."

Why Does This Matter?

The toddler years are the time when children learn to stand up for themselves. Some children take things away from others and some children are willing to let that happen. By letting one child continue taking something from another, one runs the risk of creating bullies and victims. It is the adult's responsibility to teach children assertive language and attitudes so they will be able to stand up for themselves in appropriate ways.

COMMON BEHAVIOR AND NORMAL DEVELOPMENT:

Toddlers live in the "here and now," so "now" is the only temporal concept that has meaning for them. Using the word "now" helps to explain and support the development of their concept of possession *e.g.*, "She has it now, so it is hers," or "You have it now, so it is yours."

Toddlers are also in the egocentric stage of development; they perceive the world as revolving around them and everything in it belonging to them. It is natural and common for toddlers to take things away from other children. Every "possession" incident is an opportunity for the adult to encourage sharing. One can share something of which he/she has possession. Sharing must be voluntary and therefore must be modeled and described many times.

Allowing a child to take things from other children unchecked gives them a sense of power over others that, in turn, can lead to bullying. Adults need to help children feel in control of their lives. For toddlers, this may mean saying "yes" or "no" to sharing and asking for what they want.

ATTITUDES THAT CREATE CARING COMMUNITIES:

✦ "If people take things away from you, I will give you the language and support to stand up for yourself."

SKILLS FOR CONSCIOUS EVERYDAY RESPONSES:

+ Intervene whenever any child takes a toy away from another regardless of that child's reaction

+ Let children know that no one can take something away from them unless they give it to them

+ Always model sharing as a voluntary action

IF YOU NEED MORE:

Other conscious ways for the adult to stay objective and rational:

If Marie goes back to Carrie and takes away a toy, the adult moves quickly between the children and says, **"Marie, I know you want to play with this toy now, but remember that it is not yours if Carrie has it."** Marie will probably become angry, so when giving the toy back to Carrie, say, **"I'm giving this back to Carrie because she had it first. Let's go find something to play with that can be yours."**

If Marie continues to take toys away from other children, an adult needs to shadow her and intervene quickly when another situation arises.

Our Game

Watching Children's Competence Unfold

SITUATION:

Akira and Mike, 33 and 34 months old, are running and pushing plastic shopping carts down a fenced-in walkway. The boys are shouting and laughing. They stop as they approach the end of the walkway, barely touching the wall with the carts. They repeat this over and over without bumping into each other or crashing into the fence or the wall. After watching the boys, Gina, also 33 months old, grabs a cart and joins in the fun. The three children continue this game for a few minutes.

COMMON ADULT RESPONSE:

"Mike! Akira! Gina! You are going too fast. Slow down before someone gets hurt."

Conscious Adult Response:

Caring and Descriptive Language:

The adult is aware that the game could be dangerous behavior. However, instead of intervening immediately, the adult takes a moment to observe what is happening. After watching the game, it becomes clear the children's behavior is not dangerous. The first caring response in this case is silent observation.

As the game ends, the adult describes the children's behavior: **"Wow, Mike, Akira, Gina, you were really going fast, but you stopped the carts before you hit the fence or the wall. Mike and Akira, you let Gina play the game with you. I heard you laughing and screaming. It looked like you were having fun playing your game!"**

Why Am I Doing This?

✦ The adult is fulfilling his responsibility to keep children safe by staying close by and observing silently. Observation reveals that the children have created a game with rules that they follow, which keep them safe. By not intervening, the adult gives the children the message that he has confidence in their ability to play their game safely.

✦ Describing how the boys shared and accepted Gina into their game, and describing their laughing and screaming, gives them the language and meaning for sharing and happiness.

CONCEPTUAL FRAMEWORK:

Child's Point of View:

"I can create my own game that is fun and safe."

Why Does This Matter?

When an adult shows confidence in children's ability to create games and play safely, the children gain a sense of competence. They believe they can create their own games, make their own rules, play cooperatively and receive the support and confidence of the adults they care about. This situation supports their need for independence from adults. The silent, attentive adult who remains close to the activity gives the toddlers the assurance and comfort they need.

COMMON BEHAVIOR AND NORMAL DEVELOPMENT:

Toddlers normally seek independence, but also approval and comfort, from the adults they care about. Sometimes that approval is not direct intervention, but being silently attentive. Toddlers need to make lots of noise, have ample space in which to run, and situations to practice the control of their bodies. Toddlers have a long attention span and persistence when an activity involves something meaningful and interesting to them. Finally, it is normal and necessary for them to do things over and over again to master a skill.

ATTITUDES THAT CREATE CARING COMMUNITIES:

✦ 'I will be watchful to support your independence and creativity, and intervene only to keep you and your friends safe."

SKILLS FOR CONSCIOUS EVERYDAY RESPONSES:

+ Be a silent, attentive observer
+ Describe the actions that express happy feelings
+ Trust children to be competent
+ Be aware of a toddler's need to be independent and connected at the same time.

IF YOU NEED MORE:

Other conscious ways for the adult to stay objective and rational:

If the game becomes dangerous because the children run into the wall or fence, the adult would stop the game and describe what is happening: **"When you run and crash into things with the carts, that is not safe. You might get hurt or break the cart. Show me how you run and stop before you crash."** If the children don't stop crashing the carts into things, the adult must stop the game and redirect the children, *e.g.*, set up an obstacle course for them to push the carts through, discuss with them what they could put into the carts, etc.

If the game becomes dangerous because the children run into each other, the adult would stop the game and describe what is happening: **"You are running into each other with your carts. This is not safe. Someone could get hurt. How can you play the game without running into each other?"** Support the children's suggestions for playing the game safely, or redirect as mentioned above.

Suggested Reading

Bailey, Ph.D., Becky A., Joan Weaver *(Editor)*.
I Love You Rituals. Harper Collins Quill
Publishers, 2000.
ISBN: 0688161170

Gerber, Magda, Joan Weaver *(Editor)*. ***Dear
Parent: Caring for Infants with Respect.***
Resources for Infant Educators, 1998.
ISBN: 1892560011

Gonzalez-Mena, Janet, Dianne Widmeyer Eyer.
Infants, Toddlers, and Caregivers, *Fifth
Edition.* The Free Press, Mayfield
Publishing Company, 2001.
ISBN: 0767416848

Gonzalez-Mena, Janet. ***Multicultural Issues in
Child Care,*** *Third Edition.* Mayfield
Publishing Company, 2000.
ISBN: 0767416856

Greenman, James T., Anne Stonehouse. ***Prime
Times: A Handbook for Excellence in Infant
and Toddler Care.*** Redleaf Press, 1996.
ISBN: 1884834159

Honig, Alice S. *Secure Relationships: Nurturing Infant-Toddler Attachment in Early Care Settings.* National Association for the Education of Young Children, 2001.
ISBN: 1928896030

Lieberman, Ph.D, Alicia F. *The Emotional Life of the Toddler.* The Free Press, Simon and Shuster, Inc., 1995.
ISBN: 0028740173

Slaby, Ronald G., Wendy C. Roedell, Diana Arezzo, & Kate Hendrix. *Early Violence Prevention: Tools for Teachers of Young Children.* National Association for the Education of Young Children, 1995.
ISBN: 093598965X

Additional Resources

THE NATIONAL ASSOCIATION FOR THE EDUCATION OF YOUNG CHILDREN (NAEYC)

1509 16th Street NW
Washington DC 20036-1426
1-800-424-2460

www.naeyc.org

RESOURCES FOR INFANT EDUCATORS (RIE)

1550 Murray Circle
Los Angeles, CA 90026
(323) 663-5330

www.rie.org

ZERO TO THREE: THE NATIONAL CENTER FOR INFANTS, TODDLERS AND FAMILIES

2000 M Street NW, Suite 200
Washington DC 20036
(202) 638-1144

www.zerotothree.org

CIPO   CMPO   CTPO

Our *Creating Caring Children* posters are a perfect
complement to this book. Each of the bright, beautifully
designed posters has been created specifically for either
infants, mobile infants or toddlers. The posters are a
concise, colorful reminder of the skills and attitudes that
nurture children and provide a caring, supportive
atmosphere in your childcare center or home.

Since 1980, the Peace Education Foundation has provided
the best in conflict resolution and mediation materials and
training. With dozens of curricula, posters, CDs, videos
and training programs available, the Peace Education
Foundation can help you establish or support a conflict
resolution program in your early childhood center, school,
community, business or home. To order the posters or to
receive a free catalog, call 1-800-749-8838.